Suffering
in
Silence

FRANCES A. MORGAN

Suffering
in
Silence

A Survivor of Childhood Abuse and Trauma

Frances A. Morgan

Fulton Books

Fulton Books, Inc.
Meadville, PA

Published by Fulton Books 2020

ISBN 978-1-64654-818-7 (paperback)
ISBN 978-1-64654-819-4 (digital)

Printed in the United States of America

Contents

Acknowledgements

I would like to acknowledge my prayer partners and supporters:

My loving husband Pastor Dale H. Morgan, grandsons Dale Morgan Photographer, Eric Morgan Jr. my beautiful daughter Dalwonderla Morgan, Eric F. Morgan Sr., Morgan E Williams and Scott P. (my Publication Assistant).

Thanks to all for helping me bring my Autobiography to life.

Introduction

I was on a journey to find out why there was so much pain in my mothers life that caused my mother to severely abuse me as a child and as an adult.

I didn't realize how severe the abuse affected me, until I wrote the accounts of my life down on paper, I discovered that my four siblings would never acknowledge the abuse still to this day. By covering up the abuse my mother so viciously did to me.

My wish is for this book to bring awareness to the seriousness of childhood abuse, and how a person may not ever forget the pain and suffering of being abused.

I hope that all who reads this book will be encourage to speak out immediately!

Frances A. Morgan

Chapter 1

THE BEGINNINGS

December 19, 2019

Go ahead! Cry and then rejoice!

This is my story told my way, cry and rejoice!

I don't even know where to start, so I guess that I will start like most people who finally sit down and try to put their childhood memories on paper.

There is so much that needs to be told, and I don't want to leave anything out.

So here it goes.

I was born in the spring of 1949 to the parents of Lucy Mae Thomas Adkins and James Jefferson Adkins. I was born in Dallas, Texas at Parkland Memorial Hospital on April 30, 1949. My parents named me Frances Ann Adkins.

I was the second child of four siblings, all of whom were born in Dallas, Texas, at the same hospital.

My nickname "Fetches" was given to me by my grandma. When she wanted me to bring her something, she would say fetch me this or that instead of bring me this or that. However, my siblings could not pronounce Frances Ann, so they would say Na-Nan.

My father was born on December 13, 1928, in Forney, Texas. His birth name was James Jefferson Adkins Sr. He was the third of thirteen children. His parents were farmers.

My father was tall, dark, handsome, and smart. He was also a lady's man, so I was told.

My mama was also smart and could have accomplished a great deal in life; however, that was not her fate.

My mama was born on March 21, 1929, in Forney, Texas. She also was the eldest of thirteen children. Her mother and father were sharecroppers. They were good Christian people that tried to raise their children right.

When my mother went to school, she showed great academic skills. She could have become anything she wanted to become, but she had to drop out of school in the sixth grade to help with the care of all her twelve siblings.

There was just no time for her to study or attend school. This left her disappointed and sad because she loved school and was a good student.

Chapter 2

SEPARATION, SUPERSTITIOUS AND TRAGEDY

My mother longed to get away from all the chores of taking care of babies, washing diapers, cooking, cleaning, and ironing the clothes.

So when she and my father started dating for a while, he asked her to marry him, and she said yes.

She knew all about his reputation with the ladies. Nevertheless, she was eager to get away from all the chores of caring for children and everything that came along with it.

She accepted the proposal because he loved her, and she loved him.

She would brag on how she did not have sex with my dad until she married him. She would say, "That is how I landed him, and those other women didn't."

Besides, my father had two children, a boy and a girl by two different women, before he asked for my mother's hand in marriage.

When they married in the spring of 1947, they moved to the south side of Dallas called the Bottom, known as Oak Cliff.

One year later, they had their first child, a boy in the spring of 1948. They named him after my father, James Jefferson Adkins Jr.

The next year in the spring, my mother gave birth to me, the first girl. They named me Frances Ann Adkins. Then every year after they had a female child, my mother bore my father four children in their short marriage together.

However, my father's womanizing ways never stopped, and my mother had to depend on my grandparents for their help and support of us for a while.

I was told that my dad liked to dress from head to toe in expensive clothing, nothing but the best, and those women didn't mind getting him anything he wanted.

My parents separated for a short while, and my mother was eight and a half months pregnant with my baby sister during that trial separation period.

During that time, our family lived with grandpa and grandma and all her siblings on the farm.

During this same time, my father constantly begged my mama to return home with him because he loved her, and he wanted so desperately to reunite our family, especially since she was carrying his fourth child.

She refused because of her pride. She just would not return to her husband.

One day, my grandparents and Mama went to the grocery store, and while buying groceries for the whole family, my mother spotted my father there with another woman getting groceries.

Well! My mother had a fierce temper, and she walked up to that woman and emptied her basket of grocery to the floor, knocking her down and out. She then hit and kicked my dad until the store owner, my grandpa, and my father held her so my mama would not hurt the unborn child she was carrying.

Well, this woman got up and put a curse on my mama and the unborn child.

The woman pointed her finger at my mother and said, "That's all right because the child you are carrying will never get along with you. That child will always be at odds with you and you with her."

I guess my mother believed that curse because she was superstitious.

It was my baby sister that gave me the information about the curse; however, she said that Mama had told her this story many years ago, and she said that the curse was on me. Mama was pregnant with me instead of her!

However I was born two and a half years before my fathers death, mama was lying to my sister when she told her it was me that the curse was on. She was really pregnant with her, the curse was never on me but on the both of them!

My youngest sister pleaded with me not to tell my mama that she revealed this information to me, she said that if I did she would just say that she never said it, so I promised her that I would keep it between us two.

My mama was superstitious, and she didn't want that stigma to be on her beloved baby girl, so she just turned that whole curse around on me. In her crazed mind, she wanted me to be the one that would never get along with her, and we would be at odds with one another.

She told that lie so long that she believed it herself. Or did she?

You will know just why later on in the story.

My father, who was still separated from his pregnant wife and always in and out of work, had finally landed a good job a short time later. My mama was in her ninth month and about to deliver.

My father thought this is the time for him to try once more to get his family back together again.

He hurried back to the farm to give her the good news of him landing a good job. He told her all about the pay, insurance, and vacation time that he would have and how all their bills could easily be payed now, and she and the children will have the things they needed and wanted. She agreed to take him back, and they could try to live their lives as a family again.

My father worked for the Florescent Light Company in down-town Dallas, making a decent income. The family was about to get back together and be on the right track when only two weeks on that job, my father accidentally touched a live wire and was electrocuted to death.

This tall, dark, handsome, smart, and academic young man was gone, deceased, in the prime of his life.

Although my father never finished high school, nevertheless, he had a high IQ, fast in training to work any job, professionally or manual labor. He just loved the ladies.

It devastated my mother when she finally got the news.

She took the funeral hard because of the separation, and she was about to deliver the baby.

Look at the whole picture! There she was, a young widower, twenty-three years old, and now right back in the same place where she tried so desperately to get away from.

Children! Children! Work! Work! And back on the farm with her parents.

She probably felt that it was some kind of cruel joke. She was very superstitious.

She never thought her marriage would end with her husband and our poor father's accidental death.

My father died when I was only two and a half, so I remember little about him, only what was told to me by my mama, cheap gossip, family members, seeing all those family photographs, and, as I stated earlier, what my younger sister told me about that curse!

There were nineteen people staying in that three-bedroom-frame farmhouse in the country once again.

When I was very tiny, I remember seeing or dreaming that I saw a man's face that looked like my father's face, and I thought I heard his voice, but I couldn't figure out if it was a dream or reality.

Chapter 3

LIFE ON THE FARM

My mother never forgot the woman that put the curse upon her and her baby because she is, to this day, superstitious. Nevertheless, she thought if she showered the child with lots of love and respect, telling her how much her father loved her, and how he wanted to see her face growing up but died before she was born, she thought the curse would just go away.

So she set out to do just that. My baby sister could do no wrong. However, she was a sweet child that never gave me any trouble. You see, I had to help with the care of all my siblings.

Mama thought she had to make up for the curse and the fact that my father never got the chance to see his baby girl.

She had a lot of crazy guilt to bare.

I have always known and heard that my mother was very short-tempered, but her behavior became more and more strange and weird to me, and I could not figure it out.

She acted like she hated me. She did not treat the other children with shame and disgust, but she did me.

I could do nothing right. She called me stupid, slow, ugly, and lazy.

When she felt I needed scolding, her face changed into this foul, hateful and disgusted look as she walked toward me. I knew I was about to get a slap in the face, hit with her fists, knocking me to the floor and kicking me while I lay there.

I just could not figure it out. I was no older than five and a half, closed to six years old by now, when I noticed the hostility that she had for her father and some of her siblings. She started getting along bitterly with her siblings and father. My mama would say that she loved her mother and didn't mind letting everyone know it, but she couldn't stand her daddy.

Around the same time, within weeks, I can't remember just when it happened, but my brother James Jr. opened a bottle of Bayer baby aspirin. He ate the whole bottle and nearly died. This caused him to have a weak heart, and later, he developed a small hole that should be repaired with open-heart surgery.

As I grew older, my mother grew crueler and crueler toward me.

She started working by cleaning houses, taking care of white children, making a little money, and saving it to move away from her parents on the farm.

I enjoyed living on the farm. My grandmother would see that they fed and clothed us. And we went to the Little Red Brick schoolhouse for schooling. I liked all the farm animals, helping with planting crops and taking them to the market in my grandpa's hay wagon that he would sometimes let us all tag along in.

We all had a pet farm animal. I had a chicken, my brother had a horse, and my sister had a pig.

Not one of my uncles or aunts graduated from high school, and some of them would tease us because we had to live with them because our father had died. They would say, "Yawl aren't going to get none of our something to eat. Our daddy bought this food for us, and yawl can't have none."

They would say this every day. We would sit at the table to eat dinner, and every time I heard it, I would get so angry, I would cry. Then one day, my grandma overheard what they were saying to us.

Then she politely said to them, "You have your daddy with you, and they don't, and it is not their fault. You all have plenty, so when we eat, they eat because the Lord has blessed us with more than enough, so we can share."

Then she said to those nasty kids, "Don't you ever let me hear you say such a trifling thing again."

My grandma could always make me feel wanted and loved. She had a loving spirit for everyone she met.

The boys worked the farm with my grandpa, and the girls had a little schooling, but not one of them graduated from high school.

One day, one of my uncles came to me and said that he wanted to toddle diddly me—meaning, he wanted to have sex with me. Then he said, "If you don't, I will tell your mother that you did something bad, and you know what she will do to you. You know how she is." I was only five years old, and it still haunts me to this day.

I believed him because I was so afraid of what my mother would do to me. All she needed was any old reason to punch on me!

So it got to be a habit that this is what he would say to me. I was so young that I did not understand what was happening.

As I think back over the molestation, I am convinced that some middle uncles coached him into molesting me.

Because I remember one of the middle uncles approached me, saying, "I want to do with you what he did" I ran and hid in the closet all day, and no one could find me!

He never bothered me again. I thought maybe the middle uncle threatened the younger uncle into molesting me by lying to Grandpa on him and get him in deep trouble.

The same way, he came to me and said that he would tell my mother lies on me.

People need to understand just how a young child predator mind works through manipulation of any circumstance in that child's life to get just what they want from the small child.

It takes everyone to be aware of people! Our teachers in the school, the church, neighborhood, close family, close friends, anyone who will just take time to look for signs of a child that is being molested.

There are truly signs, just have concern for our children, and let your heart of love and concern be your guide.

My grandpa would keep those boys in line. He would beat them with anything he got his hand on when they got out of line or disobeyed him. That's why I feel that if Grandpa had known about what that uncle did to me, I think he would have really hurt all who was to blame.

I know this now; however, I did not know it then.

The three oldest uncles were the ones I looked up to. They were good uncles, and I liked only one of the older aunts. The rest were not good to me at all. They had favorites, and I wasn't one of them.

It really didn't matter because the one aunt that I liked was the best one. She got her education. She was successful and married with children to a good man.

Nevertheless, I was not afraid of Grandpa at all, but I was horribly afraid of my mother, so I convinced myself to tell no one, not even that special aunt that I liked, and she liked me.

That uncle that violated me was about fifteen now, and he was always getting himself into serious trouble with the law—robbery, breaking and entering people's houses to steal, getting into fights, accused, tried, and convicted of rape.

He raped some women at White Rock Lake, he and his gang of hoodlums. The married women were at the lake with men that were not their own husbands. The men were deacons in the church, and they were at the lake having sex with the women.

That uncle and those hooligans he was with robbed the men at gunpoint, then they locked them inside the trunk of their cars while they stripped those women of all their clothing and raped them, leaving them naked in that park.

I guess they thought they had the right to do such a horrible thing because those men and women were committing adultery, who knows the mind of Satan.

They were all identified and caught a very short time later, and because that uncle had always been in and out of juvenile and jail for similar crimes, he was sentenced to life in prison.

I thought to myself, *Now is the time to tell my mother just what he had done to me when I was around five and six years old.*

There was so much gossip about the rape and robbery on the lake by this uncle that everyone in the family had their own opinions about it.

I was around fourteen years of age.

I overheard my mama talking to some of her friends about the ordeal, and they were all in favor of that uncle, her brother, and those thug friends.

My mother said she believed her brother because she asked him if he did really rob those men and rape those women.

He said he didn't do such a thing and that she knew him better than that.

My mama then said that those women were nothing but hoes. They were all married, and they were all committing adultery!

"They are the ones that should go to jail!" she said. "All of them are lying on those boys. I wish that they would all go to hell for lying on my brother!"

It was then that I knew that I would never tell her about him violating me, so I never told a soul. It was my secret that I thought I would take to my grave!

I felt like just screaming at the top of my lungs!

I cried and cried in silence.

Yes, only God and I knew about it until I got married, and I shared that horrible secret with my husband.

I never told my mother or anyone in the entire family.

I just blocked it out even to myself, but it always came flashing back from time to time to terrify me.

That uncle was released from prison only to die from some terminal illness within a few months.

I am not for sure, but I think that is why they released him from prison after they locked him up for so long, and now he would be no threat to the public because he was dying.

That is my opinion.

Chapter 4

EMOTIONAL BREAKDOWN

My mother finally got a small settlement from my father's death on the job, along with an insurance policy.

With this money in her hand, she bought a little three-room house on the south side of Dallas. She also purchased a car. Things were changing for her, and she seemed happy.

I wanted to tell her all about the molestation, but I was so afraid that she would not believe me, and she would kill me and bury me in the backyard or something worst. She would say things like that to me to control me, keeping me horrified of what she could do to me.

We all started school in the city, and I just couldn't get the learning process started. I found it very easy when I attended kindergarten and first grade in the country.

I liked that, but public schools in the city were difficult for me.

I became self-conscious because, at the country schools, I was in first and being promoted to second grade; however, the city school put me back in the first grade, having my sister and I enter the same grade together. I was told that the same thing happens to students that went to private schools and Catholic schools.

I could never live that down, but my brother had no problem with it.

I felt shame, with no one to speak up for me. They made fun of me. They would say, "Which one of you failed the first grade?" I would fight at the drop of a dime when they made those remarks.

I don't know. Maybe I was just acting out all my frustrations about the trauma I experienced back on the farm and knowing the resentment my mother had in her heart for me.

My mother acted oddly again. I know now that she had a lot of pressure on her with taking care of four children, house note, utilities, a car note, and only one income.

I remember one sunny cold day, my great-grandpa had all four of us children outside sitting on the front porch with warm blankets around us, reading to us the story of *Hansel and Gretel* when this big ambulance drove up backward in the front yard.

Then the men all dressed in white went into the house and brought my mother out on a stretcher. I noticed her wrist was all bandaged up, and I saw a little blood on both of her bandaged wrists!

My papa said, "Don't worry and be still."

"Where is mama going? What's wrong with my mama?" I screamed and yelled so loud that my ears popped!

They all knew, but no one ever spoke of that again.

I know now that she had a nervous breakdown and tried to commit suicide by slashing her risks with a razor blade.

I was only six and a half, but that memory stays with me always.

Chapter 5

MAMA PREGNANT

She got better. Then she started dating married men, four of which I know of personally because I lived my short childhood and teen life with all my mother's drama with married men!

The first married man was the man she had a child by. It was a boy. He looked like a little round pumpkin, so we gave him the nickname pumpkin.

I remember my mother going ballistic when she found out that man was married and that she had gotten herself pregnant by a married man.

She cooked him a big turkey for dinner and invited him over to have a family dinner. She fixed his plate, and he politely said, "No, fix the kid's plate first."

She had already told us not to eat anything. She would feed us later.

She told him, "We already had dinner. Because you had gotten here late and the kids were hungry, I fed them sandwiches."

He then told her to eat first. She cursed him out and ordered him out of her house.

She took that turkey and threw it into the trash.

Later on, I found out she put poison in the turkey.

She would not let that man see his child, and she drilled into our skulls that there is no such thing as a half sister or half brother if the mother gave birth to all the children.

I didn't know if that was true science or not, and I never questioned that theory either.

She loved that child, but she hated the father.

I would get into many fights if someone called him my half brother.

My mother was very partial toward the two youngest children.

When I was about eight, I asked her, "Why do you beat and curse me? You don't hit or whip the others like you do me."

My mother looked me in the eyes and said, "The baby girl, her father died before she was born, and the baby boy, well, his father will never get the chance to raise him if I can help it, so that's why I have to make up for them." Then she would say, "That's why, you little hoe!"

I was old enough to understand that everything was all about her. She controlled everything.

She finally dated the second married man. He was one of the head deacons in the church that my grandparents attended, and people respected him. He had nine children.

She dated this man off and on for about eight years. I did not like this man. He seemed to be sneaky and dishonest, and I didn't trust him, and he knew it.

Even though my mama treated me so badly, she was still my mother, and I felt that I had to love her.

I never saw them fight or argue, but I knew they did because I knew my mother and her personality. Beside she would drink hard liquor, her favorite was Colt 45 malt liquor and J&B scotch.

One day, my mother and I were out driving. My mother said with hostility, "There he is. He's following me here! Take this money, and don't let him see it."

After a few seconds, she finally stopped the car. He walked up to the window, and he said, "Give me my money!"

And she said, "What are you talking about? And why are you following me?"

Then I said, "Stop talking to my mama that way."

She said, "It's all right, Frances, give him the money!"

She did not see that man for a while, but when she started back seeing him again, she had the same old pattern of mood swing. I was walking home from school one day, and the deacon picked me up and told me my mother had an accident. I was asking many questions, and he kept saying, "Just don't cry when you see her."

When we got to the house, I ran in, shouting, "Mama, are you all right?"

When I saw her, I not only cried, but I also screamed as loud as I could! They said that the gas oven had exploded in her face. She looked like a mummy to me. Her face and hands were in white gauges. Everyone said it was an accident. She was trying to light the oven, but I knew in my heart that she tried to commit suicide again.

Things were still not right with her and the deacon so he stop seeing her for a couple of years.

Chapter 6

BAD KARMA

Then she met a big, ugly, light-skinned, married man. This man scared me to the core. He had bad karma. He stood about six foot two and 230 pounds.

I can say that I hated that horrible man.

He was just as mean and cruel as Mama was. They both drank. He would drink cheap liquor like Thunderbird and White Lighting. He would not hold a job. He was lazy, and he would beat her, giving her black and bloody eyes.

My mother would scratch his face deep and bloody, kick him in the groin, fight him with anything she could find that was heavy.

I once saw her kill a mouse with a hammer.

Sometimes, he would eventually overpower her only because of his statue. I must have lost my mind because I ran up to him and said, "Why don't you just leave my mama alone? I hope you'll die!"

Nevertheless, she could stop him with an ice pick or a knife. Then later on, she started carrying a gun.

She could always protect herself. Yes, she could hold her own, cursing and arguing and always prepared for the fight.

I would sneak and call my grandpa and tell him, "They fight all the time, and he hurts her." This got me in trouble with him and her.

My mother never wanted her parents to know about the men in her life. She told me, "You better not tell anyone what's going on in my house."

From that time on, that man did everything he could to get me in trouble with my mother so he could give me a whipping with an ironing cord. I remember having a scab on my hand, and he would hit me on that hand, knocking the scab off, causing the wound to bleed.

Other times, he would scare me by driving fast in his old raggedy Ford pickup truck, where the door flew open, and I thought I would fall out.

My mama would not leave him when they fought like that, and I could not understand why just like I never understood the thing she would say and do and tolerate from those men.

That man scared me, so I wet the bed. I hated him, and I wished him dead. He whipped me with ironing cords for wetting the bed, and he would always say, "I will beat you every time you wet that bed, and it will be with all your clothes off the next time."

I could not stop wetting the bed no matter how hard I tried, so I kept getting whipped with ironing cords naked, and my mother said nothing. She just let it happened. She was so horrible.

We would go to the park on the weekends and play.

Well, he went with us as a family outing, but he had other things in mind for me.

He knew that I enjoyed swinging on the swings, but I was afraid to go high. He came over and pushed the swing high so he could hear me scream, hoping that I would jump or fall out and hurt myself.

He did that one time too many. When my mother came over and asked him to stop because I was afraid, he then said, "I do not scare her. She is just pretending to be afraid," with a loud and hateful voice.

My mother knocked the hell out of him. Nevertheless, I paid for it later because when I wet the bed again, he whipped me, and he would say, "So I scare you hum."

This man would whip all of us kids except my baby brother and baby sister. He really took a shine to my baby brother. He tolerated the other two. However, he disliked me and didn't care if anyone knew it, but he did not want my grandpa or my uncles to know what was going on behind closed doors. He was the perfect gentleman in front of my grandparents.

He would bring them gifts and always address them with Mr. and Mrs., yes, sir, and yes, ma'am.

Our neighbor had three big pear trees, and they would let us kids pick as many pears as we could carry. One day, I picked and ate too many of those pears, which upset my stomach. When I went to bed that night, I thought I had to pass gas, but it was diarrhea.

My mother pulled back the covers and pulled me out of bed by my hair, hit me in the head with her fist, and then wiped my face and hair in the feces.

She ordered me to get out of her face, and that man said, "You need to whip her tomorrow with this whip." They kept a whip hanging on the wall.

I hated that man, but I also hated my mother. She was so disgusting to me.

I wanted to just run away, but I didn't know where to go. We were in the city now, and my grandparents still lived in the country.

I felt so helpless, afraid, and confused. My mother was like a monster to me, and she would let a man treat me with this kind of indecency.

Mama always ordered me to call no one, not even the neighbors. I felt so alone, and I asked God to let me die.

That man could fool my grandparents for a while, but he could never fool my uncles one bit. I think they were waiting for any chance to beat him up. Somehow they knew that he was rotten.

I was talking to my favorite aunt when we visited them one weekend on the farm. I told her how the two of them argued and fight with ice picks, knives, and their fists. I told her he beat me for wetting the bed and how much I hated him.

She told all my uncles right fast and in a hurry. They said to me, "Okay, the next time he hits you or your mother, call us, and we will fix him." They were the three oldest uncles still living and working on the farm.

Now remember my mother has always had a love-hate relationship for her father, and she felt resentment toward her sisters and brothers because she thought her father did not love her but love them.

There was gossip about her having fair skin, long hair, and very smart in school, so people didn't think she was her father's child.

The brothers and sisters were around her age, never went to school, and the youngest never finished high school because they all had to work in the fields on the farm.

The brothers could not attend school because they worked on the farm and helped with the work around the house. The younger ones attended school but never graduated.

Mama really didn't look too much like them, and I believe she was mentally ill and treated differently by her relatives. They gave her the nickname "red gal" because she was light-skinned and had shoulder-length hair, and her siblings were all dark skin and had coarse hair.

I think she held a grudge from being teased and gossiped about for so long, her siblings would say things like our daddy is not your daddy taunting her saying red gal, red gal, our daddy is not your daddy, and mama said that the adult relatives said similar things to her as well, when she was a child.

My mother had a love-hate relationship with her father. So I asked her one time, "Why do you go over to visit them then?"

And she would say, "I only go to their house to see my mother. I love Mother. She can do no wrong, but I can't stand Daddy."

When we got back to the house from visiting my grandparents, that horrible man asked me what we talked about, and I said nothing. He got angry and said, "Tell me what you said."

I was frightened and said, "They don't like you, just like I don't like you because you beat up on my mama, and you beat up on me!"

He put me on punishment and would not let me have dinner. I sneaked on the phone and called my uncles, and they were there within an hour.

My mother and that man were arguing when my uncles rang the doorbell. They did not wait for the door to be opened. They just broke in and dragged him out. He tried to run, but they all jumped on him.

He was begging and pleading for them to stop kicking and stomping him. He said that he would never do it again. I could see that he was just a big coward. I thought to myself, *You can fight my mama and beat me with an ironing cord, but with a man, you run and cry like a baby.*

Then I shouted, "Don't stop beating him, please! Kill him! Kill him!" while crying and screaming at the same time.

They beat him up real good. They warned him to never put his hand on their sister and her children and told him they knew that he had abused all of us.

They said that if they saw or were told by anyone that he was at the house or near the house again or ever again, they would surely kill him.

Mama stopped seeing this man finally, and I think it saved her life and possibly my life.

Chapter 7

MAMA DRAMA

Nevertheless, she started seeing the married deacon again, and she never stopped drinking alcohol.

I felt that it was only a matter of time when the cold-blooded monster would fully return with all the cursing, hitting, kicking, biting, and telling me I was the worst child she had and how I won't amount to anything because it was all my fault that her life is the way it is. "You ugly bitch, you will never get married because you are a lazy liar, and if you marry, he will leave you barefoot and pregnant all the time."

When I was in junior high school, I enrolled in band class. I played the clarinet, my favorite instrument, and I was good at it. I worked for my aunt, earning enough money to buy a clarinet.

I loved to play "Greensleeves." It would calm me down when I was angry or sad. One day, I was practicing a new song in the house, and before I knew it, she knocked me out of my chair onto the floor. She was screaming at me, saying, "You stupid bitch-ass-hoer! Get in the backyard and play that shit! You are too loud!"

We had a big collie dog named Teddy. He was a gentle dog that would not hurt a fly, and I loved that dog. I said, "I had enough! I'm running away!" You see, by then, my grandparents had moved to the city, and they lived only one mile away. So I ran to my grandparent's house, crying, and Teddy following me every step of the way. I had to pass by a nightclub, and there were drunk men outside as I passed by.

Teddy started growling, barking, and slobbering, and I heard those men say, "Let's get her and drag her into the car." Teddy crouched down and growled, then the men said, "We better get out of here because that dog will tear our asses up!"

While I was crying, running, then walking, and running out of breath, I started remembering all those times that my mother had abused me with her cruel words, how I couldn't concentrate on schoolwork, how I dislike the teachers that ever spoke in a harsh tone to me, how she beat me, how she read a magazine of horror to me, telling me how a man cut his wife's head off and cut out her pelvis, put it in his pocket, went downtown, and threw her head in the garbage can.

For years, I thought someone would cut my neck, and I would self-consciously hold my neck all the time. I really don't know when I stopped doing that. I recalled how she never believed my side of anything, how she attended none of my plays in elementary school, how I was the one that had to take care of everything at the house, how I seldom would play with the other kids, how I had to make sure the work was completed and the kids was clean and fed so she could get off one job and go straight to the beauty college she attended, how I had to wash and rinse clothes by hand and hang them outside to dry barely reaching the clothesline, how she let every man she ever met whip me, the molestation by her brother, and how she made me feel unworthy, incapable, and unloved.

Before I knew it, I was at my grandparent's house. It surprised them to see me crying and with Teddy by my side as we stood at their door.

With shocking words, I told them how my mother had knocked me out of the chair for playing my clarinet inside the house too loud. And that is why I was running away because I couldn't take it anymore.

My loving and protecting dog then left me with my grandparents and headed for home because he knew that I was in safe hands. Dogs are truly our best friends.

I told my grandparents for some strange reason that I remembered when my brother got into some baby aspirins, and he ate the whole bottle, causing his heart to be weak, leaving him with a small hole in his heart.

I remembered feeling resentment and hatred.

I remembered her affairs with married men, the beating, the abuse that came out of her own mouth, the fighting in school, having no support group, seeing my mother wrist when she tried to kill herself, the fear every day and night by the men she brought into our lives, knowing that my mother doesn't love me enough to protect me, and she was the one that hurt me.

I told them everything, only leaving out the molestation because their son was the one who molested me.

My grandpa immediately called her, and he said, "Lucy Mae! Where is Frances?"

She said, "I don't know. I guess she is outside in the backyard."

He said to get her. I could hear her calling my name over the phone. When she came back to the phone, my grandpa interrupted and said, "She is here with her dog, and I want to know why."

I think my grandpa always knew that something deranged my mother, and he learned to deal with her.

I could hear her screaming, saying, "You mean to tell me she has my dog over there with her?" Then she said, "Never mind! I'm coming to get her." When she got there, she said, "Frances is a liar. She is mean and wants to have her way! Now I'm telling yawl, she is my child, and I'm taking her home!"

My grandpa said, "Let her spend the night here, and you can come and get her in the morning."

She said, "Fine. You can keep her for all I care because she is nothing but trouble."

Then grandpa said, "Now you can see what I had to go through with you."

That next day when I went back home, she told me she had to sell my clarinet. I cried for days, and later on, I found out that one of her best friend's daughters needed a clarinet, and she gave her mine. I was only grasping for answers to why all this was happening to me for so long in my short life as a child and teenager.

Years have passed, and I guess I blocked out much of my horror while I was a child. Now I was about thirteen.

My mother and the deacon broke up for good this time. He whipped my sick brother with an ironing cord naked, and he grabbed me by my hair and held me up against the wall.

We were teens by now and going through puberty, not taking so much abuse off her men anymore.

However, my mother continued to drink and abuse me for any old thing.

Chapter 8

A KIND HEARTED
MAN FOR MAMA

She met the last and only married man this time in her life. He was a kind man, and he truly loved her. He was trying to get his divorce so he could marry her. In the process, she became pregnant, but she had a miscarriage.

This caused her bouts of depression, and she drank heavily. She really loved this man, and he loved her, and most of all, he loved all of us, her children.

It was not long after the miscarriage that she began her old ways of cursing like a drunken sailor, wanting to fight him, crying, and feeling sorry for herself, and he sat her down and told her just how much he loved her and the children. He told her that if she didn't change, he would just walk away and give her some space, but he would never leave her. He was a good man. By now, I was about fifteen.

He and I could talk, and I trusted him.

I understood him, and he understood me regarding my mother.

It was like God sent this man into our lives.

He could see that she never would take the time to help me with my homework. She never would talk with me or even teach me to play a game of cards, but she would with the others.

He would say to her, "Baby, you are wrong. Stop treating her like she doesn't exist," but she just kept on with her shenanigans.

I didn't miss out on love and affection because my beloved grandmother gave me plenty of that.

Grandma would always say, "I love you, fetches, so you love yourself too."

I truly felt loved by her, and everyone she ever met loved her too. She was an angel here on earth just for me.

Well, I finally got very good at school with my academics. I played in the band and was popular because of my sense of fashion. I wore swoop-up hairstyles, swing-out dresses, and go-go boots. I was good in track, softball, and volleyball. I also enjoy listening to the Temptation—"My Girl," "Marvin Gay, What's Going On," "Smokie Robinson," "Tears of a Clown," and "Shop Around." My favorite movies were *The Ten Commandments, The Bad Seed,* and *Who's Afraid of Virginia Woolf.* My favorite TV shows were *77 Sunset Strip, Flip Wilson,* and *Mr. Topper.* Just when things were going so well, I became pregnant halfway through my senior year.

In high school, fortunately, that boy and I did not make it. When my mother found out I was two months pregnant, she tried to beat the baby out of me. She said that her daddy and everybody would talk about her. She kicked me in the stomach and busted my lips. I ran to the bathroom and locked the door. She just broke that door in like it was nothing, and she hit me with her fists, hitting me in the stomach until I coughed blood. She then closed the door and left the house with all my sisters and brothers.

God was with me because he saw my pain and the baby wasn't hurt, and God bless me to meet a good man. It was like I knew this man all my life. We told each other everything, and the first day I met him, I told him I was pregnant. He said, "I don't care. As far as I am concern, the child you are carrying is mine because I love you, and I love the child you are caring."

I was only eighteen, and the man that really loved my mother gave my husband my hand in marriage, and my husband really thought highly of him also, and he called my husband a real man.

This man stepped up in place of my father, and I will forever be grateful to him for that. He was truly another angle in my life.

I graduated from high school, went on to city college, and gave birth to our first child, a girl. A year and a half later, we had our second child, then seven years later, we had twin boys.

My mother became pregnant again around the same time that I was pregnant with my first child. It was sad to say, but it was another miscarriage by the same man that loved her.

She never tried again, but she had a strange fixation to my daughter, stating that her child would have been the same age as my daughter.

It led me to believe that she felt that my child was hers.

I am sad to say that the loving man that helped my mother and was good to all of us passed away two years later, but he never stopped caring for the whole family.

People, I can now see that God just wanted me to know that he was with me all along and wanted me to grow and be a strong woman.

It was still sad to say that my relationship with my mother has never changed. It had been up and down for years, and at the time of this passage, she was still drinking, smoking, angry, and attempting to kill herself.

And I still ran to her rescue, and she still resisted it with all that is within her.

My aspirations in academics were to attend Baylor College of Dentistry and become an orthodontist, to get married, and to have children; however, two out of four were not bad.

By this time, my grandpa had just passed away, and somehow my mother stopped smoking and drinking, but she still had her devilish ways. However, the next chapter is waiting to be told because this chapter happened over twenty-five years ago.

I know now that I can conquer fear, shame, and hatred with God's help.

Chapter 9

FAMILY BLISS & THE
REVELATION OF HEAVEN

My husband and I had our first house built in 1970. We were married only one year with one child and eight months pregnant with another child. We were nineteen years old.

We built the house with love. It had three bedrooms, two baths, a small living room, a living den, a kitchen, a breakfast room, and a one-car garage with a big front yard and backyard.

We were happy and blessed.

My first job as a working mother was at Merrill Lynch Pierce, Finer & Smith. I sent orders of stocks to different places in America. I worked there for three years. Then I worked at Floyd West, later became Crum and Foster Insurance Co. I was a case examiner for three and a half years there. Then at Parkland Hospital, I was a nurse administrator for three years, Blue Cross and Blue Shield for four years as an account executive, and Pearle Vision Center as an office manager for three years.

I got burnt out doing office work, so I enrolled myself in Nelson Beauty College, where I earned my Cosmetology License. I became a shop owner with a beauty supply business. We named it Frances Beauty and Barber Supply and Shop.

I never forgot my childhood upbringing and all that I had to go through. It made me sad and angry throughout my entire life.

It also gave me hope and a closer walk with God. Oh, I always had a close walk with God in all my trials. I never forgot to pray and ask God to help me even as a little child, and in a way, I think my mother knew this.

My grandparents were devout Christians, and my grandpa was the head deacon in the church that they brought me up in. My grandparents gave me a strong Christian background.

They were good people. I wish I could say the same for some of their children.

Throughout my whole life, through the good and the bad, somehow, I always knew that God was always with me. I accepted Jesus as my savior at an early age and just kept him close to my heart and mind.

I enrolled myself into as many Christian correspondence courses that I could find and studied every religion I could.

One night when I retired for bed, I fell into a deep realm sleep. When suddenly, the ceiling turned into a mural of lights, doves, angels playing their harps, and then a figure of a man that looked like the Shroud of Turin.

This figure spoke to me, and this is what he said, "I am the Lord thy God, and I have a message for you, to be meek and humble yourself before I can use you."

Then everything vanished one by one in order just as it came, the bright light faded away, the doves magically flew away, the angels playing their harps faded away, then the Shroud of Turin faded away.

Then suddenly, I found myself with a sea of people, all dressed in white robes that covered them from head to feet.

I said to myself, "What is this place, and why am I here?"

The people said nothing to me. They just stared straight ahead and with their backs facing me.

I spoke to them, "Why are you all so healthy and rich? And just what are you all staring at?"

Then I reached out to touch one, and they all parted way, then I could see for myself what they did not say.

I saw a glass platform with two figures sitting on their throne.

I knew it was God the Father with our Savior Jesus, looking on as both sat on their thrones.

There were people so vast, and they were all dressed in white. I knew right then they were the saints of God, praising him all day long.

Suddenly, I felt shameful and afraid because I felt I shouldn't be there in the presence of our Holy God.

I understood that I was a sinner saved by God's grace; however, I had not even started my service to God and to humanity.

I ran and hid from God because I was in my sinful state. Right then, I became naked and under a big spotlight. This revealed my disgrace.

I felt so stupid for trying to run and hide from God my sin and shame.

Then within a second, I found myself behind two elders. They were walking and talking together, ignoring the fact that I was there.

They were holding a very large book. It reached from heaven to earth, and I knew that it was the Book of Life.

Then the elder in the front said to the elder in the back, "Her name is written here! Her name is written here!"

Then the elder in the back jumped for joy and delight, repeating the same thing, "Her name is written here!"

Now the elder in the front said with a sad tone, "But she is not ready, and she will have to go back."

The elder in the back just lowered his head, and they both floated away.

That morning when I awoke, I immediately wrote this revelation down.

I started my routine choirs as usual, but this revelation changed my life.

Because of this experience, I knew for sure that heaven is real, God is real, Jesus is real, the Bible is real, the Holy Spirit is real, and everything that I have ever learn about spirituality is real!

Now I had this revelation over forty-six years ago, and it changed my life for the better.

Nevertheless, it is still a struggle for me to be meek and humble.

However, I am fighting the good fight of faith daily, knowing that Jesus lives in me. I may fall down, but Jesus lifts me right back up again to do the works of salvation.

I know for sure that this is the way for me to get my saintly white robe and stand before God and Jesus, not to be shameful and full of sin because as it is in heaven, so it is in me!

(France A. Morgan, written on July 7, 1973)

Chapter 10

MORE MAMA DRAMA

Jesus changed my life, and for a while, I blocked all that had happened to me in my childhood for years, and I grew in spirituality. I tried to get along with my mother and others. I succeeded with some but not my mother. Like always, she just would not let me in. Previously, it was a struggle.

I grew angry and resentful toward her again and stayed away, but I ran to her rescue when she would try her suicide shenanigans.

One day my mother called me, crying and saying that she would die and that she had all her affairs in order. She said, "By the time you get here, I will be dead."

I jumped in the car, forgetting to open the garage door, damaging the garage door. When I calmed down, I drove to her house, which was three miles away. When I arrived there, the front door was already open. She was sitting in a chair with pills in her hand and a glass of water. I looked down on the floor, and beside her, I saw a black box filled with papers. Then she said to me, "I'm taking all these pills, and I will die." She started swallowing those pills, and I tried to stop her. She bit my finger. I stopped and called 911.

By the time the paramedics got there, she was out on the floor. The paramedics came in and found me crying, kneeling by my mother on the floor. They asked me, "What is the problem?"

And I said, "She took a bunch of pills."

They said, "Who is she to you?"

I answered, "She is my mother."

They worked on her, checking her pulse, heart rate, blood pressure, rubbing three knuckles into her chest. Then one paramedic asked me if she had lost a loved one recently or depressed about something.

I answered, "No. Why did you ask that question?"

He said, "There is nothing wrong with her, and her vitals are fine. She is wide awake, with her eyes closed and blinking. She is also holding her breath. We see this in cases of mourning for a loved one that has just passed on. There is one other test that we can do, and it will surely prove that I am right. It is a smelling test. Now if she is out, she will awake right fast, but if she is faking, she will just lie here as she is."

They did that test, along with knuckling her in the chest, and sure enough, she just lay there with her eyes closed and holding her breath.

I showed them where she had bitten me on my finger, and they cleaned that bite and informed me that a human bite is worse than any animal bite and that I should see the doctor and get on antibiotics and a tetanus shot.

The paramedics left the house, and Mama got up off the floor when she knew that they had left. I just sat there, looking like the biggest confused fool ever!

I said nothing to her as she got up from the floor. She said to me in a defiant voice, "Don't you ever, as long as you live, call a paramedic to my house again. You knew that he was hurting me when he took his two knuckles and dug into my chest."

Sure enough, her chest was as red as blood.

I am so ecstatic to say that my mama never pulled another suicide attempt ever again!

Three years have passed since that day, and by then, my beloved grandpa died. All the uncles and aunts and grandma took it hard; however, my mother, I couldn't say, but she stopped drinking and smoking shortly after that.

But she never stopped her resentment toward me, and she always made a big difference between my children and her other grandchildren. Nevertheless, I tried for my children's sake to let her have a relationship with them. She brainwashed my oldest because she truly believed that she was her child, and my husband and I suffered for that choice. However, everything worked out all right for our daughter, and she is perfect with much praise to God.

One day, one of my twins pulled a little figurine off her table, and she jumped up and said, "Goddamn that little motherfucker! He knows not to mess with my things."

My son was only ten months old and barely walking.

I said, "No! God did not damn my little baby son, but he did damn you!"

She pulled a gun on me and threatened to shoot me. We left her house, and we did not see or speak to her for years.

I never told my children all the horrible things I had endured from my mother because I didn't want to traumatize them.

Chapter 11

TESTIMONIAL OF
GOD'S BLESSINGS

God blessed our family as we tried to live our lives as God-fearing Christians.

My husband made a very good living as an automobile salesman. He earned high recognition as the top salesman in the state of Texas. Received numerous awards and bonuses.

We bought a two-story home an traveled the world. My husband is a kind and loving man to everyone he meets.

He was known for being an honest auto salesman. Our family attends church and put God first in our lives.

Then two years later, we had another tragedy happen. My eldest brother James Jefferson Adkins Jr. died of a heart attack. It devastated us all; however, I know that God won't put more on you than you can bear.

When our children were all grown up, God called my husband and me to preach his Word.

We heard and obeyed the call of God upon our lives and with the Holy Spirit's help. We opened the church doors, preaching and teaching God's Word to the people.

My husband and I are working for God now because he worked for us in those hard times in our lives, letting us know that he has and will always be with us.

We don't have the money that we had twenty-five years ago, but thanks be to God, we have Jesus, and we have not missed out on anything.

Now I am not saying that the old dirty devil has not tried to touch us with tragedy, but we know that God has us in his loving care.

I have fought breast cancer twice in my life, and I know that God brought me through.

I have had many surgeries, and I know that it was God that brought me through it all. I give God all the praise because he so rightly deserves my praise.

I have such a testimony of God's love for me, and I am here today to tell the world that if God did that for me, he would surely do it for you because God is not through with me yet.

I want you to understand that God put me with the best doctors, surgeons, and oncologists.

God, my husband, children, grandchildren, and great-grandchildren are my greatest support group. Throughout the ordeal, they praise and thank God for my victory.

My loving and caring husband is going through medical issues as this book is being written.

I pray for him both day and night, and I have faith that God will bring him through with good health to preach and teach his Word for many more years to come.

My husband is a prayer warrior that loves the Lord and a man of great faith.

We both are praising and worshiping God every day, and we know that his body is well because he has the light of God living inside of him; therefore, it is well. With his soul, God will heal him in the name of Jesus Christ, Amen.

I am so proud to say that all our children are Christians. They are all successful in life, and God has blessed us with nine grandchildren and three great-grandsons.

Heaven is in us.

The next book will come soon.

Frances A. Morgan

About the Author

Frances A. Morgan is the wife of Pastor Dale H. Morgan for fifty-one years. They are the parents of four beautiful children, grandparents of nine, and great-grandparents of three. Frances and Dale are thankful to God for their family.

Frances A. Morgan is a Dallas native. She graduated from Lincoln High School in Dallas, Texas, and studied computer at El Centro Junior College. At Mountain View Junior College, she studied creative writing and psychology.

Mrs. Frances A. Morgan was the owner of Frances Morgan Beauty and Barber Supply for four years. She received her cosmetology license at Nelson Beauty College in Dallas, Texas. Frances received her bachelor of arts degree in 2007. Later on, she received numerous awards and certificates at D. Edwin Johnson Bible Institute in Dallas, Texas. Frances was inspired by God, her loving husband and children who pray for her constantly. Frances A. Morgan's prayer is for everyone to receive a blessing from God by reading her autobiography and for everyone to understand that God is always there for them in all circumstances, and to never be silent about abuse of any kind it is not your fault.

So never give up on God, may God bless you all.

Now Rejoice and never lose faith in God!

Frances A. Morgan